PAS
Switzerland

Passport To The World

Passport Argentina
Passport Brazil
Passport China
Passport France
Passport Germany
Passport Hong Kong
Passport India
Passport Indonesia
Passport Israel
Passport Italy
Passport Japan
Passport Korea
Passport Mexico
Passport Philippines
Passport Poland
Passport Russia
Passport Singapore
Passport South Africa
Passport Spain
Passport Switzerland
Passport Taiwan
Passport Thailand
Passport United Kingdom
Passport USA
Passport Vietnam

PASSPORT
Switzerland

Your Pocket Guide
to Swiss
Business, Customs & Etiquette

François Micheloud

WORLD TRADE PRESS®
Professional Books for International Trade

World Trade Press
1450 Grant Avenue, Suite 204
Novato, California 94945 USA
Tel: (415) 898-1124; Fax: (415) 898-1080
Toll-free USA order line: (800) 833-8586
http://www.worldtradepress.com
http://www.globalroadwarrior.com
E-mail: sales@worldtradepress.com
"Passport to the World" concept: Edward G. Hinkelman
Cover design: Peter Jones, Marge Stewart
Illustrations: Tom Watson

Disclaimer
This publication is sold with the understanding that the publisher is not engaged in rendering legal or any other professional services. If legal advice or other expert assistance is required, the services of a competent professional person should be sought.

Acknowledgements
Thank you to Clément Bucher and Laurent Monod for their input and to Paul Bilton and Mara Bertelsen for their proofreading and other comments. Finally, special thanks to the numerous clients whose observations about Switzerland have been included in this book.

Library of Congress Cataloging-in-Publication Data
Micheloud, François-Xavier, 1973-
Passport Switzerland: Your Pocket Guide to Swiss Business, Customs & Etiquette / François-Xavier Micheloud.
p. cm. -- (Passport to the World)
Includes bibliographical references.
ISBN 1-885073-88-7
1. Corporate culture--Switzerland. 2. Business etiquette--Switzerland. I. Title. II. Series.
HD58.7.K527 2001
395.5'2'09494--dc21   2001017710
                                                              CIP

Printed in the United States of America

Table of Contents

Switzerland

Switzerland
Quick Look

Official Names	Confederatio Helveticae
	Helvetisches Bund
Land Area	41,285 sq. km, 15,940 sq.mi.
Capital	Bern
Largest City	Zurich (pop. 336,821, 1998)
Elevations	Highest: Mt. Rosa 4,634 m
	Lowest: Lago Maggiore 193 m

People

Population	7 million
Density	171 per sq. km
Distribution	68% urban 32% rural
Annual Growth	+ 0.2%
Official Languages	German 63.7%
	French 19.2%
	Italian 7.6%
	Rhaeto-Romanic 0.6%
Major Religions	Roman Catholic 46%
	Protestant 40%

Economy

GDP	US$214 billion
Foreign trade	Imports: US$71 billion
	Exports: US$72 billion
Principal trade	EU 63%
partners	Germany 23%
	France, USA 10%
Currency	Swiss franc
Exchange (3/01)	1.65 Swiss francs = US$1

Education and Health

Nobel Prizes	19
Infant Mortality	4.8 per 1,000 live births
Physicians	187 per 100,000
	inhabitants (1999)
Life Expectancy	Men: 76.2 years
	Women: 82.3 years

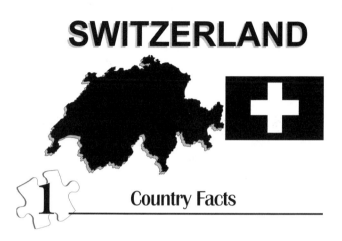

SWITZERLAND

1 Country Facts

Geography and Demographics

Switzerland is one of the smallest countries in Europe. It is also one of the most crowded. Shaped like a piggy bank, two thirds of the territory consists of scarcely populated mountains. Cities and industries are concentrated in the banana-shaped plain that stretches from Geneva to Zurich, a densely populated area where most of Switzerland's 7 million inhabitants live.

The Birth of a Nation

Switzerland had a rough birth. Napoleon brought the French conception of a centralized state in 1798 when he invaded the country and christened it as "The Helvetic Republic". But this system did not work for the Swiss, and the French emperor had to change it in 1803: the Mediation Act sanctioned the principle of a federal system with then 19 cantons. After Napoleon's defeat in 1815, Swiss neutrality was officially recognized by the European powers. In the decades that followed, the liberal bourgeoisie clashed with the conservative. After a short civil war in 1847, the Radical Party (Liberal) came to power and gave Switzerland its constitution in 1848.

At the beginning the Swiss did not share much in common, as they spoke many different languages and were divided by religion and custom. However, they had a common mistrust of the powerful states that surrounded them.

Nowadays, the cohabitation between the different groups functions quite well compared to countries with similar cultural differences such as Belgium or Canada, even if from time to time some political clashes occur between the Swiss Germans (the majority) and the Swiss French (the minority). A recent example happened with the national vote for the entry of Switzerland in the EU in 1992, where the German-speaking Swiss refused despite the enthusiasm of a majority of the French-speaking Swiss for the new European order.

Foreign Population

There are 1.4 millions foreigners living in Switzerland (20% of the total). They are an essential component of the economic and demographic balance of Switzerland's aging population. In fact, without its foreign residents, Switzerland's population would decrease by 7,500 every year through death and emigration. However, thanks to the foreigners' higher birth rate, the total population is actually increasing. Immigrants are attracted to Switzerland by the quality of life and some of the highest salaries in the world. However, with such a high foreign population, immigration is a constant issue in Swiss politics. Strict federal immigration regulations apply, with annual quotas and a strong bias in favor of European immigrants, who constitute almost 90% of the foreign population. Swiss citizenship can be obtained only after 12 years of continuous residence, a police inquiry and a Swiss culture exam, which sometimes includes the recipe for fondue (see Chapter 19). As a result of these strict controls of the country's foreign population, xenophobia is very low and violence against foreigners non-existent.

Climate

Some people imagine that Switzerland is as cold as Alaska, but this is far from the truth. In the plain, temperatures can rise to 30°C (86°F) in the summer, and even in the mountains the sun is hot. In the winter, temperatures rarely drop below minus 5°C (41°F) in the entire country, save the mountaintops.

The mountainous character of Switzerland is responsible for spectacular differences in the weather among different regions. It is very common to move from a cold, cloudy and rainy landscape to a beautiful clear blue sky with hot sun in just a few minutes. The warmest parts of the country are Montreux (where palm trees line the lakeside), Ticino and Valais.

In Ticino, the Italian-speaking canton South of the Alps, there are over 298 sunny days a year and daily mean temperature in July are over 26°C (79°F). In Valais, kiwis, peaches, figs and tomatoes are grown in orchards and tiny scorpions can be found.

Business Hours

Offices generally begin their day between 8 A.M. and 9 A.M. and close between 5 P.M. and 6 P.M., Monday to Friday.

Shops usually open at 9 A.M. and close at 6:30 P.M., Monday to Friday, and are open from 9 A.M. to 5 P.M. on Saturdays. Lunch breaks are quite common in smaller shops, usually from noon to 2 P.M.

There's growing pressure to keep shops open later in the evenings. In train stations, airports and service stations, you can find some shops that stay open till 10 P.M.

Government offices have widely different opening hours. Some open at 7:15 A.M. while others (generally smaller) open at 9:00 A.M. Lunch breaks are the rule, with people leaving the office from 11:30-12:00 A.M. to 1:30-2:00 P.M. While published closing time is between 4:00 and 5:00 P.M., you may find it difficult to find anybody after 3:00 P.M.

National Holidays

The following holidays are legal holidays all over Switzerland:

New Year's Day (Neujahr/jour de l'an/capodanno): January the first.

Good Friday (Karfreitag/ Vendredi Saint/Venerdi Santo). First Sunday after the first full moon after the Spring Equinox (late March).

Easter Sunday and Monday (Ostern/Pâques/Pasqua) : Second and third day after Good Friday.

Ascension Day (Auffahrt/Ascencion/Assensione) : 40 days after Easter Sunday.

Whit Sunday and Monday (Pfingsten/Pentecôte/Pentecoste) : 10th and 11th days after Ascension Day.

National Day (Bundesfeier/fête nationale/festa nazionale): August the first (Celebrates the Oath of 1291, which is considered the start of the Swiss Confederation).

Christmas Day and St. Stephen's Day: (Weihnachten/Noël/Natale): December 25 and 26. Note that St. Stephen's Day is not always a holiday, as it often depends on company's good will.

Federal Fast (Bundesfast/Jeûne federal): Second Monday of September except in Geneva where the Genevan Fast is celebrated on the first Thursday of September. Don't be mistaken; these two dates are occasions of feasts rather than fasts.

Cantonal Holidays

Individual cantons recognize a wide range of local holidays to honor saints or to commemorate a battle. They are too numerous to list, but here are some non-working days valid for most Catholic cantons:

Corpus Christi (Fronleichnam/fête Dieu/Corpus Domini) : 60 days after Easter Sunday.

Assumption Day (Maria Himmelfahrt/Assomption/ Assunzione): Not to be mistaken for the Ascension, which is when Jesus goes to Heaven. This time it is his mother the Holy Mary who goes.

All Saints Day (Allerheiligen/La Toussaint/Ognissanti): November the first, also known as "The day of the Dead."

Immaculate Conception (Maria unb. Empfängnis/ Immaculée Conception/Immacolata Concezione): December the 8th.

As an example of the rich diversity of Swiss cantonal customs, here's a typical cantonal feast celebrated in one canton only:

L'escalade (The climbing): Every year on December the 12th, the Genevans celebrate their victory against the Savoy invaders who attacked their city the night of December the 12th, 1602. The heroic and ultimately successful defense of the city included such highlights as the *Mère Royaume* pouring hot soup over soldiers climbing the city walls. People gather in the streets dressed up like their ancestors, offering soup and hot wine, and children are offered small and sometimes big chocolate caldrons filled with candies to commemorate the soup that saved the city.

The Swiss

A Multilingual Land

The Swiss come with three languages as standard equipment: their mother tongue (i.e. Swiss German, Italian or French), another national language that is not their mother tongue and English. This makes the Swiss equal to the Dutch in terms of linguistic ability, but in Switzerland it is just taken for granted.

The main languages of Switzerland are German (or rather Swiss German), with 65% speaking it, French (20%) and Italian (7.5%). A few thousand people in Grisons speak Romansh, the closest living offspring of ancient Latin. It has recently been promoted to the status of an official language for the sake of regional cultural recognition, but has no practical importance.

Good news for speakers of English: the English language is widely understood in Switzerland, especially in the German-speaking part and in Geneva. The Swiss are indeed so fond of English that many advertisements are in English, which has the double advantage of being hip and of avoiding the need to translate everything three times.

Swiss German is not German

The Italian and French spoken in Switzerland are very close to the languages spoken in France and Italy, with some differences in accent. Swiss German is another story altogether. A Germanic dialect, it is almost never written as people use *Hochdeutsch* (High German) for writing. Since it is only spoken, it is fast evolving, with numerous colorful expressions that are great fun when you understand them. For example, the Household School for girls is the *Rüebli Rekruten Schule* (the carrot boot camp).

Pronunciation is akin to Dutch but more guttural, with many sounds coming from uncharted quarters of the rear of the throat. If you want to have fun with Swiss friends, ask them to pronounce *Chuchichäschtli*, Swiss German for the "little kitchen cupboard".

Being justly proud of their language, the Swiss Germans are often reluctant to speak in High German, perhaps because they are troubled by hearing Germans speak it so fluently. They often prefer to speak English rather than German.

Bad news for those who want to learn Swiss German, as this language varies widely from one area to another and there's no standard orthography. The best strategy for visiting English speakers is to ask, "Do you speak English?" and look relieved to find they do, very well.

Religion and Ethics

Switzerland is divided into 26 cantons, whose borders often mark religious and linguistic areas. Most cantons were created with either a Protestant majority (like Geneva and Zurich) or a Catholic one (like Valais, Fribourg and Lucerne). Where two communities share the same territory, cantons are divided into half-cantons. For example, Basle City (Protestant) and Basle Country (Catholic). Mentalities vary greatly, according to factors such as religion, language and whether people live in town or the country. Thus, people from rural, Catholic, German-speaking cantons have a very different mentality from those living in Geneva.

Even though people are hard working, motivations for working and the general attitude toward life is not the same. Among the 30% of "authentic" Genevans in Geneva, what matters is money in the bank rather than indulging in spending. Parsimony, modesty and long term views are the rule and make Genevan businessmen a prosperous bunch. Apart from saving and investing, the Genevans will feel strongly obliged to give money to charities (of which there's no lack in Geneva). This mentality is skillfully described in Albert Cohen's books (*Solal, Belle du Seigneur*).

In Catholic, rural areas, people are not inhibited at all to spend their money for expensive cars or Texas-sized houses, and feel a duty toward their family at large. Corporate paternalism and nepotism are seen as values. Family and quality of life tend to be rated higher than profit, especially when people have worked hard enough above basic needs to be wealthy by their community's standards. Those who build corporate empires are seen as lacking common sense, and the point of piling up many times more money that one can use is not understood. These differences in *Weltanschauung* exist even among people who are not religious in the least.

Honesty is the rule among the Swiss, and for a very practical reason. The Swiss do not need to work themselves into an early grave to make a nice living, but one act of dishonesty can tarnish a reputation and make life much harder. The moral of self-interest can thus partly explain the scrupulous honesty of most Swiss.

The work ethic is strong throughout Switzerland, but the reasons for this vary. In Protestant cities like Zurich or Geneva, the driving force is morality, the conviction that only those who work hard will be redeemed (read Max Weber), whereas in rural and Catholic cantons, where poverty ruled only 50 years ago, working hard has always been the only way of surviving for the mountain peasants. Today, people are much better off, but the ethic of hard work remains strong.

Education

Many countries have abandoned any hope of an efficient state education system long ago, but not Switzerland. Teachers are respected, and well paid. A high school teacher can earn up to Sfr.9,000 a month and there is a long waiting list to become one.

The school system works so well indeed that even top government and business leaders send their children to state schools.

Children begin with primary school only at age six. Based on the marks they get in their last year of primary school, they will go on to different types of secondary schools. Technical schools prepare pupils for manual occupations, whereas secondary schools lead to apprenticeships, and high schools (around 10% of the students) prepare for university. Most enroll into apprenticeship programs at 15 or 16, with a mix of weekly specialized and general classes and on-the-job training. After two to four years, candidates must pass an exam to obtain a Federal Certificate of Capacity for their trade.

At the end of high school (around age 18 or 19), the *Maturité* diploma is awarded (akin to the *Baccalauréat* in France or *Abitur* in Germany). Most then go on to study at university. Graduate titles command great respect in Switzerland and are readily displayed on business cards. The university attended is not very important, the Swiss being not so sniffy about those things.

However, Switzerland being Switzerland, every canton has its own syllabus, exams and vacations.

Too Much Democracy?

Anyone who does not believe that you can have too much democracy should be sent to Switzerland. Gather 100,000 signatures and you can put to vote a change in the constitution. If 50,000 citizens decide so, they can block any law passed by the Swiss Parliament and have the entire country vote on it. This works for small things too. Don't like the new multimillion shopping mall project down the street? Any resident of the neighborhood can delay it for months with a simple letter explaining why it will lessen the quality of life.

But people are not crazy about the power the system gives them. With votes and polls taking place every two to three months on a vast number of municipal, cantonal and federal issues, voters get tired of their duties and the turnout is usually 30% or less. Perhaps there can be too much of a good thing after all?

The Swiss political system may be slow, but it is stable and efficient. For a constitutional change to be passed, both the majority of voters and that of the cantons are needed. In practice it means that a tiny canton the size of an Edelweiss (e.g. Uri, with 36,000 inhabitants) will weigh in a federal vote with as much clout as Zurich (1,181,000 inhabitants). As the smaller cantons are not the most liberal, the balance swings in favor of conservatism.

By balancing power among the regions in a

very generous way, this system has kept Switzerland united for 150 years, preventing its many linguistic, religious and economic divisions from tearing the country to pieces.

For readers with an interest in political institutions, some places in Switzerland are worth a visit. In the small, scenic village of Gruyères (yes, home to the famous cheese), citizens gather twice a year in a communal assembly to vote by raising their hands on municipal issues. Or the picturesque canton of Appenzell, where until recently even cantonal issues were voted upon with raised hands by a general assembly of men, the *Landsgemeinde*.

Low Profile Government

Swiss politicians are not in the same league as the politicians of its bigger neighbors. Swiss citizens with a taste for power usually find it more rewarding to engage in business rather than politics. Not that Swiss politicians are absolutely powerless, but power is so well divided between municipalities, cantons and the Confederation that nobody enjoys much say over anything.

A Rich Swiss is Redundant

Measured by income per capita, the Swiss are the richest people on Earth. Some resented this leadership and tried to impose another measure of national wealth that would take into account the cost of living (PPP GDP). By this criteria, the richest are the Americans, and the Swiss come third. Whatever the truth is, in Switzerland, you won't notice much of this wealth displayed. Apart from the highest number of Rolls Royce and Ferraris per capita in the world—many of them owned by foreigners—people make it a virtue to keep wealth discreet. In Geneva, children are shown the example of rich private bankers who go to work either on bicycle or with the bus, living statues of Calvinist virtue.

How the Swiss View Themselves

The Swiss are convinced that their wealth and the stability of their prosperous country is due to their hard work and nothing else. And who can blame them? During the 19th century, Switzerland was one of the poorest countries in Western Europe, a land of meager farming and no natural resources. Many Swiss emigrated during those years, creating cities like Nova Friburgo in Brazil or New Glarus in the US.

During the 20th century, and especially after the 1950s, the country began to develop almost as quickly as Japan. Today, Switzerland has the lowest inflation and unemployment rates of all industrialized countries, the highest income per capita, and the second lowest interest rates. The crime rate is among the lowest in the world and most of it is committed by foreigners. The last time Switzerland went to war against another country was in the 15th century (apart from a brief civil war in 1847).

Swiss success has become a standard for small countries that do well: Lebanon was once called "The Switzerland of the Middle East" and Chile the "Switzerland of South America."

National Identity and Pride

Every nation likes to think highly of itself, and the Swiss are no exception. Swiss national pride does not show itself in military parades and demonstrations of international supremacy, but rather in the quiet conviction that *Y'en a point comme nous* (There are none like us).

This superiority complex is reinforced by most statistics and observations from foreign visitors. You will not make a big hit complimenting the Swiss on the beauty of their landscapes. However, you will please your Swiss acquaintances greatly if you learn something about the few famous Swiss. Here are some examples:

Henry Dunant, was born in Geneva in 1828. A wealthy Calvinist businessman, he turned philanthropist after visiting the battlefield of Solferino and helped create the International Red Cross and the Geneva Convention (1864). Dunant's life went from riches to rags (declared bankrupt in 1867) and back again as a result of his charitable pursuits. He received the first Nobel Peace Prize in 1901 for his efforts.

Cesar Ritz, was born in 1850 in Valais and emigrated to Paris to learn the restaurant business. Coming up through the Parisian restaurant hierarchy, he finally came to open his own Palace, which has been known as the Ritz ever since.

Karl Gustav Jung, a founding father of modern psychoanalysis was born the son of a preacher in 1875. After having been Freud's right hand for years in Vienna, he became increasingly critical of the Freudian school and developped his own theories from 1913 on.

Louis Chevrolet, born in 1878 in la Chaux de Fonds, was so fond of race cars that he created the Chevrolet Motor Company in 1911 in the US.

Le Corbusier, born Charles Edouard Jeanneret in 1887 in the same city as Chevrolet, became known as a concrete loving architect and urban planner all over the world. One of his most striking projects was the planning from scratch of Chandigarh, an Indian city, where he was able to test his theories on a large scale.

Alberto Giacometti, born in Ticino in 1901 first studied in Geneva and then began a sculptor's career in Paris. Most know him for his long, skeletal bronze statuettes such as the Pointing Man (Tate Gallery, London).

For good measure you can add **Albert Einstein**, who although he was born in Germany (1879), lived for years in Switzerland where he first developed his theory of relativity while moonlighting in the federal patent office. Einstein obtained his Ph.D at the University of Zurich and was later appointed as a lecturer at the University of Berne.

Attitudes Toward Other Cultures

For many Swiss, there are two kinds of foreigners: those who bring and those who take. Free-spending Arabs and their successors, the new Russians, business people and the rich tourists who flock to Switzerland all belong to the first category.

Refugees (Switzerland has the highest rate per capita of political refugees in Europe) are the main category of those foreigners perceived to be net "takers", as well as, unfairly, some seasonal workers who come from Mediterranean countries to do work that the Swiss do not want themselves, such as cleaning, waiting on tables, and building roads.

Some cultures and countries stand out, especially the USA, which commands a great fascination among younger Swiss. The USA is all that Switzerland is not: big, homogeneous, not bothered by ancient hierarchies, a land of competition. Americans are the second biggest visitors to Switzerland after the Germans and they are appreciated, even though every Swiss can tell a few horror stories about culturally illiterate American tourists. Superficiality is a common cultural stereotype associated with Americans among the Swiss. This perception is enhanced by the common use of first names by Americans.

In French-speaking Switzerland, Parisians have

the reputation of behaving like rude colonists, thinking they are coming to an underdeveloped country where everybody has a cow and speaks like the actors on French TV commercials for Swiss cheese.

The EU attracts mixed reactions. Basically, the majority of French-speaking Swiss are in favor of joining the EU, whereas the German-speaking part rejects it. "What is in there for us?" they ask pragmatically. Switzerland would loose its Swiss franc, loose control over the borders, perhaps even loose its neutrality and, most important of all, loose money.

The Swiss National Hero

Who might the national hero of such a peaceful and wealthy land be? A banker probably. Or maybe Henri Dunant, the Geneva banker and founder of the Red Cross? No, the Swiss have elected a man of the people, William Tell, whose head graces the 5-franc coin. Tell lived in Uri, when it was ruled by the Austrians. The bailiff Gessler, local representative of the Austrians, used to place his hat on top of a wooden pole in Altdorf so that every passer-by could greet it in a sign of obedience. William Tell and his son passed by without paying their respects. Gessler ordered their arrest and offered him the following deal: "They say you are good with the crossbow. I will put this apple on your son's head. If you can shoot an arrow through the apple, you will be free. If you refuse or fail, you will be hanged." The apple was placed on his son's head and Tell's arrow pierced right through it. The bailiff, disappointed, noticed that Tell had concealed a second arrow under his shirt. "What is this arrow for?" asked the bailiff. "If I had missed the apple and killed my son, this arrow was for you," answered Tell. The bailiff's men arrested Tell and put him on a boat to take him up to a dungeon on the other side of the Vierwaldstättersee (Lake of Lucerne).

In the middle of the lake, the boat was overtaken by a storm (Opera buffs: Rossini's *William Tell* Overture). The bailiff unchained Tell, who was an expert boatman, so that he could bring the boat to shore safely. Once again, Tell lived up to his reputation and made it to a safe haven, where he quickly jumped off the boat and kicked it back out into the lake, leaving the bailiff to his fate. Gessler survived and Tell realized that with him alive, neither he nor his family could ever live in peace. He killed the bailiff in an ambush.

Farinet

If the legend of William Tell (for this is only a legend) illustrates the spirit of independence the Swiss have against foreign rulers, the story of Farinet will testify to that of the cantons.

Farinet (born in 1845) was an active counterfeiter in one of the most stubbornly independent cantons, Valais. His coins were recognized by the locals as being counterfeit, but they used them nonetheless. Many people did not like the new federal authority and if they were offered an alternative to the young Swiss franc (created in 1850), they were eager to use it. Farinet minted about 100,000 coins and was always on the run, but people from the Martigny area protected him. To them he was a hero and, even during his life, Farinet was the subject of many songs and even carnival parades.

The game went on for 15 years, but this is no legend, and Farinet was finally found dead in the mountains in 1880. Did the police shoot him? Was he betrayed by a woman? We do not know, but if somebody shot him, he left the SwFr5,000 bounty on Farinet's head unclaimed. The anarchist became the hero of a book by the famous Swiss writer C.F. Ramuz, *La Fausse Monnaie*, and enthusiasts promoted him to the rank of Valaisian hero.

Cultural Stereotypes

Always on Time

The Swiss are always on time.

If there is a value that is shared by everyone in Switzerland, it is that of punctuality. Trains arrive on time, likewise the payment of bills, and people even turn up early. A German word best describes the epitome of Swiss punctuality: *Uberpünktlichkeit*, "over-punctuality", when people come 15 minutes early to be sure they arrive on time. This is far from uncommon. This may have to do with the clock industry and with Protestantism, which, by the way, was brought about by the Huguenots (French Protestants seeking asylum in Switzerland from persecutions).

Cold and Serious

The Swiss are cold and serious.

It is quite possible to spend two hours in a Swiss train in front of somebody your age and he or she will not dare strike up a conversation. It's not that your traveling companion wouldn't enjoy talking with you, but the idea of starting a conversation with a stranger seems unnatural.

Regional variations are high. Take Geneva with its 37% of full-time foreigners, not to speak of visitors, and understandably you will need more than to say you are a tourist to trigger an outburst of warmth from a local. But head for the mountains and people may well invite you to come over to drink their homemade cellar wine (many Swiss make their own wine).

Chacun chez soi – chacun pour soi (Each in his home - each for his own.)

The Swiss are an individualist lot.

"Everybody takes care of his own business and the cows will be well guarded," is a Swiss saying. People do not like to get involved in others' problems and things are usually kept within the family. A common saying is *On lave son linge sale en famille.* (One washes his dirty laundry in the family.) People will assume that if you are in trouble, it must be because you have done something wrong and until you prove the contrary, they will not interfere. Not that their hearts are made of stone, but remember that this is a people who had nothing but mountains and poverty going for them a hundred years ago, so they just don't blindly except everything to come from the state or from others. *Aide-toi et le ciel t'aidera* seems to be the motto (Heaven helps those who help themselves).

Obsessed with Cleanliness

The Swiss like things clean.

Before the days of modern Singapore, Switzerland was hailed as the paragon of clean countries. The Swiss like things clean and they do everything they can to keep spotless streets, restaurants and offices. People who want to put a TV antenna on their roof must ask the local council for authorization because it could make the neighborhood look bad. A French phrase sums up how the Swiss prefer things: *Propre en ordre* (clean – in order).

Tight on Rules

The Swiss are very rules oriented.

An American expatriate explained that one night he was crossing a street in Zug with absolutely no traffic in sight when he was stopped by an imperious old lady who reminded him that when the traffic light is red, one should wait. When he complained that waiting for the green light when the city sleeps was useless, the lady answered, "I know, but *Regeln sind Regeln*, (rules are rules) and you can't bypass them."

In some businesses, especially banking, and particularly in German-speaking Switzerland, people can be obsessive about rules.

Discretion is the Word

The Swiss are extremely privacy minded.

Many rich and famous people live in Switzerland and when they are recognized on the street, people just smile and look the other way. No Swiss in their right mind would dare bother somebody to whom they had not been introduced, however famous.

Laws supporting discretion and the respect of privacy have long been in force, especially for lawyers, trustees and bankers. The banking secrecy laws are very strict and a banker who reveals information about a client to anybody but a Swiss judge with a search warrant will be fined and can be sent to prison.

Regional Differences

Switzerland is a federation of 26 partly sovereign states called cantons. Each raises its own taxes and has a different educational system, and most differ from their neighbors either by language or religion. There are significant regional differences in culture and customs, even within such a small country (the size of the US state of Tennessee).

Zurich

Zurich, a Swiss-German speaking, protestant city and canton, comes first in most business respects, as it is the undisputed economic capital of the country, where many of the biggest Swiss companies have their head office. Due to the decentralized nature of the Swiss State, however, you should not expect everything to be centered in Zurich. In fact, most of the federal institutions are in other Swiss cities: the seat of Parliament and Government are in Bern, the Supreme Court is in Lausanne and the Insurance Supreme Court in Lucerne. Thus, every region gets its piece of the action and equilibrium is preserved.

Basle

Basle, an amazingly vibrant protestant Swiss-German speaking city located right on the frontier between Switzerland, France and Germany is the country's main non-aerial freight hub. The Rhine runs through it, establishing a port of entry for goods coming from Rotterdam. Home of the Swiss pharmaceutical industry (Novartis and Roche), this culturally lively city is also a center for modern art dealers. The fact that people there are very open to foreigners comes as no surprise. All the more so because children are given for their birthday a little wallet with three compartments, one for Swiss francs, one for French francs and one for Deutsch marks.

Primitive Switzerland

The mountainous center of Swiss German-speaking Switzerland is called "primitive" because this is where it all began. In 1291, three small communities united around the Lucerne Lake.

The Rütli Oath united Uri, Unterwalden and Schwyz (which later gave name to its country in German: Schweiz) against the Austrian rulers and was the foundation of Switzerland.

This part of Switzerland is full of breathtakingly beautiful mountains, lakes and valleys and is a political mosaic of scarcely populated cantons. Some cantons understood quickly that their Spartan fiscal stance would please foreign investors and have become havens for domiciled companies from all over the world. For instance, there are already 18,000 firms recorded in the commercial register of the Canton of Zug—not bad for a population just under 100,000.

Bern

The Swiss-German speaking, protestant political capital of Switzerland and one of its biggest cantons, Bern is a quiet place, not unlike Ottawa. The people are often bilingual in French and German. Once the mightiest of all Swiss cantons, Bern now owes a great part of its importance to its central role in Switzerland's political life, and is a quiet and pleasant place even if it does not head most business people's top destination list.

Geneva

If Geneva did not think it were Paris, it would be one of the most lovable cities in Switzerland. Pity is, this beautiful city thinks quite highly of itself as the avant-garde of Switzerland.

Sharing 94% of its borders with France, Geneva (Calvinist and French-speaking) is the economic capital of a region it does not own. It is also the political center of many international organizations. This unique conjunction of internationality and its high number of palaces haunted by the rich and famous give Genevans a sense of superiority over the rest of Switzerland. And the rest of Switzerland does not often think about it, only when from time to time it has to bail out the free-spending council from bankruptcy, which happened last in the 1930s.

Ticino: the Italian part

Just about 8% of the Swiss speak Italian, they are of course Catholics and live mainly in the beautiful canton of Ticino on the southern slopes of the Alps, a stunning mix of tall mountains, breathtaking Alpine lakes and palm trees. Ticino is indeed very close to Italy, and to reach this canton from Western Switzerland, the shortest way cuts through Italy.

Liechtenstein

Although it is an independent country with a Prince, license plates and passports, Liechtenstein shares the Swiss postal and customs systems and the protection of its army, as well as the Swiss franc.

Located on the border with Austria, this tiny country of 25,000 inhabitants is, for many people, the Switzerland of Switzerland. It has decided to do away with all the unnecessary manufacturing industries you find in Switzerland. Here, many people work either in financial services or have *Treuhandbüros* (fiduciaries) to register letterbox companies. And they make a nice living out of it too, as there is more than one registered company here for each inhabitant.

The "Roestigraben"

From time to time you may hear about the so-called *Roestigraben*, that is, the "Trench of the sautéed potatoes," a hypothetical cultural divide that is supposed to separate the Swiss German-speaking part of Switzerland from its Latin parts. This sociological myth is usually told as follows: "All the power, both politically and economically, is held by the Swiss German-speaking majority. This makes the Latin (Italian- and French-speaking) parts jealous and bitter because of their powerlessness."

You may hear this story from a tourist guide striving to make a smart observation, or even from some of the Swiss themselves.

In reality, when sociologists ask people in a careful and systematic way, they find that by and large, the Swiss population tends to consider its counterparts from other cantons nice neighbors and have very little to say about how they live or what they think. Of course, you can hear people making fun of Swiss German, which sounds like a "throat cancer," or of the people in Lucerne who "will not let a pedestrian cross a road at a red light even if there's no traffic in sight," but there's neither hate nor resentment on any sizable scale. Pity then that the press blows poll results up out of proportion when the different parts of the country have divided opinions on various topics. This is exactly why the deeply federalist Swiss political institutions have been put in place—to respect regional opinions. And this system has been acclaimed the world over as the solution to minorities' problems—even in former Yugoslavia. To boot, most Swiss are proud of their system even if they don't like it when their canton losses in federal polls.

Let's be clear here: most multicultural countries in the world would be happy to see their respective communities get along as the various makes of Swiss do.

Government & Business

Government: Pervasive but Efficient

Travelers sometimes tell Kafkaesque stories about Swiss government administration. It is indeed true that you often need authorizations from many offices, which implies a lot of paperwork. But don't be misled. This is Switzerland and administration is efficient. If you do it the right way, you get what you need reasonably quickly.

Tips for dealing with the Swiss government:

- Speak the local language or ask somebody who does to act for you .
- Never be rude or impatient on the phone.
- Give your name when calling.
- Prepare a one-phrase summary of your problem and call. You will be directed to a chain of people until you reach the one you need.
- Take down the name of the person you talked to and his/her direct phone number.
- Don't call before 9 A.M. or after 4 P.M.
- If you need to fill in a form, ask them to send it and then call the person in charge of processing for any

questions on how to fill it in appropriately.

- If you need to pay a fee, do it in the way they suggest (usually cash or through the Swiss Post).
- Don't even think about bribing an official: people are well paid, honest and corruption is almost unheard of in Switzerland.

Guilds and Cartels

Switzerland is the land of oligopolies. Many professionals, including plumbers, electricians, and medical doctors are protected by a complex set of licenses, professional rules, compulsory apprenticeships, exams and a guild. Take the driving instructor: in most countries, this is a occupation any reasonably able man or women can have. In Switzerland, driving instructors unite in "professional organizations" to "foster quality in their service and thus enhance road safety." No matter how noble the formal purpose of such associations, the most visible result is financial: these organizations impose a fixed hourly price for lessons (the association's recommended price). After a few months, the fee buys you only 50 minutes. Then, the guild tries to close the doors behind itself by raising the standards of driving instructor exams, imposing a minimum age and schooling level for applicants, and trying to exclude people who are not members from working.

Migros, Thoroughly Uncapitalist

Most European countries have witnessed the great battle between small grocers and supermarkets during the past twenty years. Switzerland is no exception, and the latter have prevailed with the biggest chains being Manor, Coop and Migros. The biggest chain, Migros, is virtually a non-profit organization. It has 38 shopping centers and 499 supermarkets in Switzerland, offering normal supermarket goods at bargain prices (that is, for Switzerland) as well as many services (travel, banking, gas, fitness and language schools). As a cooperative, the Swiss own Migros and no one can hold more than one share worth 10 francs.

Self-rule

Swiss government is very business-friendly and usually only interferes in business issues in extreme cases or upon request of the parties concerned. Regulations of specific trades and industries are usually placed in the capable hands of professional organizations, which manage them responsibly, although of course in the interest of their members.

Take banking, for example. There are banking laws in the Swiss Civil Code, as well as a special law called "laws on banks." However, many important rules are left to the Swiss Bankers Association, a private professional association. In the case of anti-money laundering measures, members of the association have signed the "Convention de diligence," which describes the behavior member banks should adopt regarding their depositors and the economic origin of deposits. In the event of infraction, the association can levy fines or exclude members.

This system of partly autonomous rule is clearly in favor of business, but generally works quite well. When new issues arise (for instance, money laundering scandals and the subsequent pressure to change rules and practice), Parliament passes the minimum laws needed to satisfy public opinion and international policy needs, and the rest is left to the private professional association to sort out. Sensitive as they are to the threat of new, less flexible laws, the associations enforce stricter regulations on their members so that they can avoid new scandals while maintaining control over part of the regulatory process. The umbrella organization of all these professional associations is called the Vorort.

Swiss Bankers

For many international businessmen, doing business in Switzerland begins with opening a bank account. This is not a bad place to begin, as Swiss banks are probably the most powerful institution in the country, after the government. And, if you deposit large amounts (half a million Swiss francs is large enough for most banks), your banker will go to any length to keep you satisfied. Need a business connection? The banker will be glad to oblige. Looking to buy a Swiss watch? He will know what to buy and where. But nowadays, bankers can give the cold shoulder to people who just drop by their office. Most new clients in private banks come from third party introductions, as bankers prefer to be able to connect a new client to somebody they already trust. You get the point—friends and clients of our friends are always welcome. The problem is finding the right banker.

Swiss Money

The recent introduction of new banknotes in Switzerland is a telltale sign that entry into the European Monetary Union (EMU) is neither for tomorrow nor for the day after. The Swiss love their money and so do many other people. And indeed, Swiss bank notes are quite something: they bear so many paper and ink tricks to fool counterfeiters that the Swiss National Bank printed an explanatory brochure for each monetary unit.

The Work Environment

Law Abiding

The Swiss respect their laws so thoroughly that sometimes it verges on the absurd. You need authorization to put a TV antenna on the roof, you cannot mow the lawn on Sundays or take a bath after 10 P.M.

Schwytzertütsch: the Swiss Yiddish

If you must speak Yiddish to trade diamonds in Antwerp, Swiss German is the language to master in Switzerland. Not that the Swiss do not speak German or English. They do, and usually very well. But the Swiss Germans are so fond of their language that if another Swiss addresses them in High German, they are likely either to switch to another language or answer in Swiss German. Of course, like all Swiss, they also enjoy showing off their English to foreigners and if you begin in English, asking if they speak it, they will probably be glad to oblige.

To truly belong, however, you really ought to speak Swiss German. If you only speak English and it is apparent that you are a foreigner, the story is different, as people will be proud to show off their language skills.

Swiss Army and the Swiss Elite

If you were a Swiss man, you would be a soldier as well. Every able-bodied Swiss man must go to the army in Switzerland for 90 days (*Rekrutenschule-Ecole de recrue*) and then every 2 years until the age of 42, he must return for practice for 19 days. This allows the government to raise an army of 400,000 men, fully armed, within 24 hours, as every soldier has an assault gun in his house, complete with ammunition. But there is more to this than a picturesque democratic institution. Many CEOs of big Swiss companies are officers in the Swiss army, and this is so common that when a normal soldier is promoted to such a position, the newspapers will mention the fact. If they have spent the long weeks necessary to reach the rank (900 days to become a Captain), it is not just for the love of guns. Officers usually address each other by the familiar form *tu* or *du* and their old boy network spreads among the most powerful industries of the country, particularly in banking. Some factories are run by teams of managers who all belong to the same army Division. When the time of the biannual "rehearsal courses" comes, the CEO just exchanges his suit for assault dress and the troops follow.

But times are changing. In the past, a successful career in a Swiss bank may have implied the need to be an high-ranking officer in the Swiss army. However, over the past 15 years banks have complained that their managers were always out of the office, and the merits of advanced military training for managers is being increasingly called into question.

The Swiss Work Ethic

Switzerland was a nation of poor mountain peasants, so poor indeed that for years they had to sell their military skills to European kings waging wars. Switzerland is not poor anymore, but the economic necessity of working hard is still alive today as a moral imperative. People forced by circumstances to remain idle for a few days often complain that they "have to saw wood" or do something productive lest they go crazy.

The Swiss work long hours (1,844 hours a year), much longer than their neighbors (the Germans work a miserly 1,573 hours a year). The Americans take the cake with 1,904 hours a year.

One would think that this strong work ethic is bred by Calvinism, a very demanding brand of Protestantism that makes people very hard working (Max Weber's *The Protestant Ethic and the Spirit of Capitalism* is the classic reference here). However, the Catholic cantons work every bit as hard and feel no religious pressure at all.

Good Labor Relations

In June 1999, the Swiss Post Office introduced a brand new computerized parcel sorting system, for which they paid SwFr150 million. A problem with the software led to such a total dysfunction that for days thousands of parcels piled up in the sorting center— the computers were useless. What did the postal employees and their unions do? Instead of complaining and making Luddite speeches, they just rolled up their sleeves and worked day and night to ensure that the mail was delivered.

With the possible exception of Geneva, most Swiss would be ashamed to strike and the idea would not even occur to them. And indeed there would be grounds for embarrassment. But even if there were reasons, several factors make strikes unlikely. First, the Swiss do not get their hands dirty and you can hardly find a Swiss among the lower paid workers (waiters, unskilled construction workers, cleaners, etc.). Most of them are first-generation immigrants who either work without a valid residence permit or are just too happy to be able to live and work in the country. Striking would not cross their mind, and indeed most union and far-left activists are second-generation immigrants.

Since 1937 there has been the so-called "Work Peace Agreement" by which unions and bosses agree not to resort to strikes or lockouts in the event of labor conflicts.

Not the Land of Competition

With such a small, fragmented market, competition is not the driving force of commerce in Switzerland. Rather, it is price fixing agreements and cartels that rule, and the consumer who pays the price. Importers commonly double the price of the goods and retailers double it again. But they have allies to help maintain this system. Take a simple water faucet imported from Germany or Italy. The consumer will pay four times the factory price and the plumber who installs it will often receive a commission of 15 to 20%, to ensure that the specialist will not try to rock the boat.

No surprise that *The Economist's* "Big Mac Index" tends to give the top prize for the most expensive burger in the world to Switzerland.

Of course the vast number of oligopolies in Switzerland has been the target of federal regulations, but it seems that the Federal Cartel Commission has so few resources and such little power that it limits its efforts to the counting of cartels.

Apprenticeships

For years many top managers whose education was limited to an apprenticeship could simply rise in the ranks of the company to which they devoted their life. At the end of compulsory education (usually at 16), the apprentice starts work in a company four days a week and theoretical teaching is provided on the remaining working day. This system used to be one of the foundations of the highly skilled Swiss workforce and the industrial strength of the country; people could definitely be successful with an apprenticeship. They still can, but there is a growing prejudice against apprenticeships and without a university degree it is now difficult to get a position as a senior executive. A recent advertising campaign tried to enhance the image of apprenticeships, but the battle will not be easy to win.

Seniority

Age and time spent in a company count, and you will not find many senior managers under 40 in big Swiss companies. Big banks are the paragon of corporate conservatism with, until recently, compulsory military service for managers.

Women in Business

A Conservative Country

Switzerland is not at the cutting edge of women's progress and by and large this is not an issue in Swiss politics and society. Women have had the right to vote at the federal level only since 1971, and the last canton to include women for regional election was Appenzell in 1991. The first female Federal Councilor was elected in 1984, but resigned (see Chapter 13). But there are quite a number of women in politics now.

Ruth Dreifuss, elected in 1993 as Federal Councilor, became the first female President of Switzerland in 1999. In 1999, a second woman—the young, dynamic and attractive Ruth Metzler—was elected to the Federal Council. But it was more her age than her gender that made the news. Elected at 34, she also is the youngest person to fill this position in over a century.

The situation at the parliamentary level is comparable to that of many other developed countries. There are 24% women in the lower house and only 15% in the upper house. An initiative to impose a compulsory 50% quota in the Federal Council and in the Swiss Parliament was rejected by 82% of the Swiss people in 2000. But the conservative view that Swiss women have of themselves is even deeper. According to a 1999 Economist poll, only 39% of the 3,000 Swiss women interviewed said they thought that "women should have all the same rights as men," the second lowest proportion of the 11 countries polled (after Japan).

The Glass Ceiling

While women account for 42% of the active population, only 18% have made it to middle ranking executive, and a meager 1 to 3% have successfully integrated into top management. Margit Osterloh, a teacher of managerial economics in Switzerland, argues: "Women who want to reach the top come up against a glass ceiling. They can see the top through the ceiling, but it stops them painfully every time." Barbara Kux, executive director of Ford Europe, doesn't agree, "The one who wants to see a glass ceiling will see it… I have never seen it."

More than half of the students at Swiss universities are women, but only 5.7% of all professors, lecturers and researchers, highly respected jobs in Switzerland, are women. There is certain gender segregation at the level of career choice. Real difficulties crop up when the time comes to have a child. Some decide to put it off until later, others retire in the risky hope they can come back later.

Prejudices have not yet disappeared. In many companies, there are people who think that a mother cannot take on responsibilities, because she might have to leave at anytime to care for her child. When a young woman is hired, it is not unusual for her contract to stipulate that she must "work full time" during a specified time, meaning that she must refrain from having children during that period. Women who work part time are almost automatically excluded from positions with executive responsibilities. The few female managing directors of banks in Geneva are Americans, not Swiss.

Understandably, many women prefer to work freelance and to create their own businesses. Since 1991, the number of women working freelance rose constantly, especially in the fields of business consulting, human resources and career development.

Women Associations and Promotion

Many civic organizations, such as the Rotary or Lion's clubs, are closed to women. In their place Swiss women have built up networks such as BPW (Swiss federation of business & professional women), WIN (women innovation network) and NEFU (network of start-ups builder).

Strategies for Foreign Businesswomen

Swiss business meetings are usually formal and task-oriented, which can be an advantage to businesswomen. What matters most is expertise and professionalism. A woman who displays a high level of competence will usually be rated higher than a man with equivalent capacities.

The title Ms. has no equivalent in German or in French, and a businesswoman can expect to be addressed as *Frau* (*Madame* in French) or Mrs., whether she's married or not. *Fraulein* (*Mademoiselle*) or Miss is used only to address those under the age of 18 nowadays. So if a woman insists on being addressed as Miss, she should make that clear when she's first introduced or when she introduces herself ("This is Miss Such-and-Such"). If, despite all effort, the Swiss side addresses her as Mrs., a correction—even a tactful one—could prove awkward.

Many Swiss will shake hands with the males present but will wait until a woman offers her hand to be shaken, so be sure to do so.

8 Making Connections

Cold Calling is Useless

Switzerland's business community is a small world where everybody knows everybody else, either directly or through common acquaintances. Thus, Swiss executives are used to meeting new business partners through somebody else. Third party introductions are vital and cold calling is frowned upon.

Old Soldiers' Network

As explained in the preceding chapter, for years the Swiss army has played the role of both a school for leaders and a men-only social club, offering young up-and-coming executives the chance to meet important people during army exercises. Although this way of making contacts probably will not be available to you, you should be aware of it to understand what your Swiss acquaintance means if he tells you he is a captain of the Mountain Grenadiers (an elite unit).

Board Cronies and All That

People sitting on the board of big Swiss companies usually sit on several. A big Swiss bank that makes loans to a major firm often tries to impose one of their employees on the firm's board, to have a privileged inside view and be able to voice the bank's interests. Thus, if you are lucky enough to know a board member of some of the most prestigious Swiss companies, you have potential access to most of the others: *Tirez le fil et toute la pelotte suivra.* (Pull the thread and the whole ball will follow.) People like financier Martin Ebner, who take stakes in big Swiss companies to make the board maximize shareholder value, are not common. Swiss corporate life is much more laid-back and cooperative, and deals are usually done very smoothly.

Tips for Finding a Swiss Partner

- Find a go-between. For example your banker or a trusted Swiss businessperson will be able to help you meet the right people.

- If you know who you have to meet, try to locate somebody who is easy to approach and who knows the target person.

- Give them a way to easily "pigeon hole" you. If you have dealt with famous companies, that can enhance your credit, as will telling them whom you already know in Switzerland, especially if they are in the same industry.

- Never brag about money or big deals you made in the past, although you can hint at them.

- Always be well prepared and accurate on the facts and figures you quote.

Strategies for Success

Local Languages

Most meetings with international business people are conducted in English. In Latin Switzerland, people will be glad to speak in Italian or French if you speak either well. In the Swiss German-speaking part you should avoid speaking High German unless your host offers to, especially if you are from Germany. Saying hello in the local language is always polite, but please do not expect the locals to cheer just because you learned to say hello.

Swiss Humor

Jokes are optional in Latin Switzerland (Italian- and French-speaking parts), but they are better avoided in the Swiss German-speaking areas unless you are familiar with both culture and language.

Ten Golden Rules

1. **Be Polite** The Swiss are as obsessed with politeness as the Japanese, and your being very rich will not be seen as a substitute for good

manners. However, unlike Japan, politeness has few formal rules. If you pay respect to your host or business partner, remember to shake hands and never shout. He or she will not ask for more.

2. **Be Punctual** Why not repeat it? Be on time. Being a few minutes late is just impolite, but if you are 15 minutes or more behind schedule, chances are your Swiss interlocutor will be very angry. If it happens during the first meeting, it can compromise the whole business relationship.

3. **Be Prepared** Prepare everything you will need for meetings before you arrive. Once there, give your counterparts documents about you and your company. Be prepared to quote figures and prices and to answer in detail any question they may ask about your products or services.

4. **Be Precise** If you quote a figure, it must be exact. When you describe a project or product, you should fully grasp all its details.

5. **Don't Show Off Your Money** With so many oil princes, sport and music star millionaires from all over the world coming to stay in Switzerland, the Swiss are used to seeing luxury everywhere. Thus people will not be impressed by a Ferrari or an expensive watch.

6. **Don't Name Drop** Famous people are common in Switzerland. You will not surprise a Swiss if you have once spoken with billionaires or political leaders. Only mention it if you have some exclusive knowledge that is relevant to the topic at hand.

7. **Don't Speak Loudly** The Swiss are discreet and reserved people. They usually speak slowly, choosing their words carefully. Speak-

ing loudly and quickly will be interpreted as being over-emotional.

8. **Don't Criticize Switzerland** Who likes to hear one's country criticized? The Swiss often criticize their own country and especially to strangers, but that is not an invitation for you to do the same. Even if they will not show it, people are often very patriotic and they will never forgive you for putting them to shame.

9. **Exporting to Switzerland** If you are a middleman, some buyers will be reluctant to do business with you. An Indian exporter recounts that as soon as he said he had several nut factories in India, he had no problem meeting the buyers of the biggest Swiss supermarket. However, another Indian who sold cotton goods independently could not get a single appointment with the same people. Swiss buyers' first concern is quality. Come with your best products and be prepared to give sensible arguments to underscore their quality. Manufactured goods should come with very good after-sales support.

10. **Business Gifts** During your first meeting you can bring business gifts bearing the logo of your organization. However, gifts intended for a specific person should not bear any logo, unless the gift is of very high quality and the logo very discreet. If you want to do your host a favor, choose a restaurant in a gastronomic guide such as the *Gault-Millau* and invite him or her for a meal. Wine, chocolates and cigars are recommended but can be tricky if you cannot tell *ganache* from *Yquem*. Offering foreign chocolates to a Swiss is a cultural faux pas, even if the Swiss are more and more aware of the excellent products made in neighboring countries.

10   **Time**

In Switzerland, Time is Money

The Swiss are known to like punctuality, to the point of obsession. So, if you have an appointment with a Swiss company at 2:30 P.M., come some time in advance and tour the building to be sure you will get in at 2:30 P.M. sharp. This is especially important for the first meeting, as your Swiss partners/clients will assess how *seriös* (reliable) you are.

Deadlines are Deadlines

If your Swiss suppliers set a deadline, you can be confident they will go to every length to hold it. Conversely, if you agree on a deadline with a Swiss client, you have to comply or be rated as unserious, which means your Swiss contact will try to find somebody else.

Notes on Punctuality

The Swiss have a reputation for being as punctual and precise as their best watches. The rule is: *Avant l'heure, c'est pas l'heure, après l'heure, c'est plus l'heure* (Before the hour is not yet the hour, after the hour is no longer the hour), with the only exception being the *Quart d'heure Vaudois* where, in the canton of Vaud, people generally arrive fifteen minutes late for an appointment. It is their way of thumbing their nose at the national on-the-dot-timing.

But secretly the Swiss are very proud of their punctuality. This precision is the expression of something stronger and more profound: their national feeling towards social and political order. *Une place pour chaque chose, et chaque chose à sa place* could be the motto of this Confederation. (A place for everything and everything at its place.) A linguistic particularity, typically Swiss, is the translation of "OK" into German as *alles ist in Ordnung* (everything is in order) or to translate "tip-top" into French as *propre en ordre* (clean and in order). Even some administrative forms have an *en ordre* box to check as opposed to a simple "yes" box.

It can happen, although very rarely, if you have a meeting concerning a job, a contract, some advice or some support with a person in a powerful position, that this person arrives late on purpose to demonstrate their power. In such a case, you will wait, and wait, and wait until the person arrives in a whirlwind, hardly taking the time to apologize and, without spelling it out, makes it clear that he, being the very important person that he is, has just come out of a meeting and grumbles that he only has a couple minutes to listen to you.

As for you, always try to be punctual. The Swiss should feel obliged to be as punctual as a foreigner as a matter of honor. It would be seen as very impolite to arrive late intentionally.

Business Meetings

Early Bird Special

Swiss business people are famous for meeting very early. Meetings at 7 A.M. are not unheard of, and that is not for a power breakfast. People in managerial positions often arrive one hour before their employees (who arrive between 7:30 and 9 A.M.), so if you need to speak with them and know their direct extension, do the time zone math and try an early call.

Be Prepared

At your first meeting, you should come prepared with all the relevant information about your organization, why you are there and what your plans are. If you are vague or lack the proper documentation, people will rate you as unprofessional. And in Switzerland, as everywhere, first impressions may be misleading, but they last.

Arrive on Time

If you come late to a Swiss meeting, even by 5

minutes, this is a bad beginning. Of course, Swiss business people know that other countries have a less rigid conception of time but this is nevertheless considered rude. If, for example, you are 10 minutes late, some Swiss will make you sit a further 10 minutes in the waiting room, so take something to read.

Swiss German Style

In the Swiss German-speaking part of Switzerland, people tend to make business meetings as short as possible. You arrive, tell them what you want, they answer and after the business discussion is over, they will close the meeting. A central European businessman reports that only after the fifth meeting and having bought millions from his Swiss supplier was he invited for lunch.

The senior manager (*Chef*) will speak first and lead the show. His lower-ranking colleagues will usually speak only when told to do so, and you should not address them directly during the first meeting.

Latin Style

In French- and Italian-speaking Switzerland the custom is to take business acquaintances out to lunch (some say that is because the food is better in this part of the country). Discussions are never restricted to business topics and conversations often touch on cultural tastes, cuisine, travel, the European Community and so on. Personal and family issues are only raised by the persons concerned.

12 Negotiating Styles

That's the Price

Swiss sellers do not have a soft approach to prices, at least not when it comes to their prices. Of course there is always some room for negotiation, but it should be done with tact and moderation.

You have to understand that the Swiss people never discuss retail prices. Either they buy it at the full price or they go away (which usually means they do not buy at all because prices are the same in every shop). And most of the time they buy, which makes it a retailer's dream. If in the morning the Swiss retailer asks: "Mirror, Mirror on the wall, tell me what is the price of a cup of coffee today?" and the mirror answers "Five francs," the consumer will take it and say "That's the Price."

Let's say you received offers for the same product or service from two different companies, and the price difference was 50%. If you were to call the more expensive company's salesman and ask him if he could lower his price in the face of the other offer, chances are that you would hear, "I can't lower my prices because competitors are cheaper, *voyons* (go away)!"

In many cases, businesses have such a captive market that buys their goods at whatever price they care to name that your deal has to be really big if you want them to change their practices. Fat cats do not need to bargain.

Apart from prices, the Swiss can be remarkably flexible when it comes to commercial deals. People do not like direct confrontation and are usually ready to compromise. As in politics, they will try to find a *juste milieu*, a solution that is acceptable to everybody. Not being able to find an agreement will be considered a failure.

Quality has its Price

Although you won't find prices for Swiss export goods cheap, they will almost always reflect the highest quality available anywhere in the world and may be a bargain after all. For example, many radio journalists across the world use Kudelski Nagra (Swiss) recorders. Although expensive, the investment generally pays off many times over in service after many decades of continuous use.

Another example is the Swiss P210 handgun made by SIG, which is literally carved out of a metal block to ensure maximum durability. The result was an expensive but extremely reliable gun. Discontinued, it is now a prized collector's item but other SIG guns are so reliable, that they are used by police forces all over the world, including many US police departments.

If you want to approach the Swiss export market correctly, your motto should be "We are not rich enough for cheap goods" (since buying cheap goods will mean that you'll have to buy them again every time they break down.)

With the strength of their currency and the

high labor costs, Swiss entrepreneurs have long understood that they cannot be competitive on the low end of the market. They have chosen to concentrate on products and services of high quality and to offer the best in class.

They Won't Tell You What They Think

Do not expect the Swiss to tell you abruptly that they do not agree at all with your opinion. They will hear you out, just saying yes, yes. If they do not answer frankly to a question—or even do not answer at all—that does not mean that they do not have a perfectly clear opinion. The Swiss hate the feeling of losing time, so if they are not interested at all, they will not comment on the matter. If a Swiss takes time with you, it means that he or she thinks there are good opportunities.

Business Outside the Law

Underground Economy

You are not likely to see any of the minuscule Swiss underground economy while traveling in Switzerland on business. Taxes being low and government reasonably small, most people see no need to hide what they do unless they deal in things illegal. The worst you will see is foreigners who work in restaurants or on construction sites without the proper work permit.

Drugs, Illegal or Otherwise

Most drugs are illegal in Switzerland, but attitudes toward non-addictive drugs are changing. The Federal Surgeon's office recently declared that they found ecstasy to be rather innocuous, somewhat of a scandal for older Swiss who cannot tell lysergic acid from methamphetamine.

Marijuana and its derivatives are enjoying a boom nowadays in Switzerland, due to unclear laws that permit the culture of this robust plant for oil or medical purposes, and tolerate some shops that sell its hemp by-products. From time to time, police will raid growers and shops to remind people that Zurich has no intention of becoming Amsterdam—although marijuana may be soon legalized for Swiss residents.

More disturbing is the heroin consumption that had found its center at the Spitzplatz just behind Zurich's central station. For years an open market for drugs was tolerated there until a crackdown in 1992.

Current issues include the big competition between traditional dealers and the new Kosovo Albanian Mafia that now dominates 95% of the market in some areas. This has driven prices down and consequently reduced the traditional crimes (burglary and mugging) associated with the search for money to finance drug addict needs.

Some cantonal governments have tried methadone and needle distribution programs to reduce AIDS and to better monitor addicts. A federal vote in 1999 approved this stance.

Crime in Switzerland

Violent crime is almost unknown, and when murders are committed it is usually between asylum seekers. Like it or not, 44% of the persons convicted of criminal offences are foreigners, half of whom do not even officially live in Switzerland.

Graft and Corruption

Corruption is almost unheard of in Switzerland, and when scandals happen, they are only on scale of the country itself. Judge for yourself: one of the biggest recent scandals caused the resignation of a Federal Councilor (halfway between a Minister and the President), and the first woman to reach that level to boot. So what terrible crime did Ms.

Kopp commit? Did she receive commissions for arms deals? Or maybe she helped herself to the State's treasury? *Eh bien non*. While she was the head of the Justice Department, she learned that her husband, a wealthy Zurich businessman, was going to be investigated by the police for alleged money laundering. She called him up saying, "they are on their way" from her office. When this phone call was discovered, she immediately resigned in January 1989 (how it was discovered is another story). Incidentally, Mr. Kopp was later cleared of all charges.

Sex and Prostitution

Prostitution is legal and there are full pages of advertisements for "massages" in Swiss tabloids. Pimping, however, is illegal and uncommon. Most of the prostitutes operate independently from small studios with their cellular phones.

Swiss prostitutes pay VAT (Value Added Tax) on their services and some take credit cards. If they have a problem with a client, they will call the police to help them out. But this is as Swiss as they get. The majority of them are foreigners from Latin America, France, Eastern Europe or the Far East. Price charged include all Swiss taxes.

14   Names & Greetings

The Swiss have names that often describe one of their ancestor's occupations or physical attributes. *Müller* (miller), *Zimmerman* (carpenter). When a woman marries, she can take her husband's name, join her married and maiden name together or even keep her maiden name on its own. Thus *Ingrid Stauffacher* marrying *Jean Ducret* can become either *Ingrid Ducret*, *Ingrid Ducret-Stauffacher* or remain *Ingrid Stauffacher*. Children will be called *Reto Ducret*.

Forms of Address & Titles

All three main languages of Switzerland have two sets of personal pronouns. The most useful for business usage is the formal form (*Sie*, *Vous* and *Lei*), but you may encounter the informal forms, *du*, *tu* and *tu* used within families and close friends. If an acquaintance offers to switch to the informal form, that is a sure sign of a personal relationship beginning. However, you should not expect it before much time has passed and in any case you should never propose it yourself.

In German-speaking Switzerland, you should

address men as *Herr Bucher*, or *Frau Bucher* for women. People who hold a doctorate should always be called *Herr Dr. Schmidt*, and if you meet a University Professor (this commands much prestige in Switzerland) you are expected to use *Herr Dr. Professor Zaehringen*.

In the French-speaking part, people are usually addressed as *Monsieur* or *Madame*. Attorneys of both sexes will be offended if you do not call them *Maître* (literally: Master), and those who spent years writing a thesis will be grateful for a *Dr. Supersaxo*.

Finally, people in Ticino have taken the taste of their Italian cousins for exaggeration, and people who hold any degree should be referred to as *Dottore Casanova*. For the rest, *Signore* or *Signora* will do.

The Game of the Name

Swiss Germans always try to remember your name when speaking on the phone. Even if you cold call and briefly mention your name, they will write it down and at the end of the conversation you will hear a nice "Goodbye, Mr. Wilkinson." This custom is not common in other parts of Switzerland and as a foreigner you are not expected to play the same memory game.

Greetings

People shake hands a considerable number of times in Switzerland, and if you meet a small party you are expected to shake each person's hand while looking him or her in the eye.

In German-speaking Switzerland, to say hello you can use *guten morgen* (good morning) before noon, and *guten tag* (good day) or *grüetzi* (hello) all day long. To say goodbye you will use *Auf Wieder-*

sehen (to the seeing again) when leaving a meeting, but *Auf Wiederhören* (to the hearing again) when closing a phone conversation. Aren't the Swiss a precise lot? The use of the local word for hello (*Gruetzi, Guetzach,* etc.) will sound strange unless you can speak at least some German.

In the French part, use *bonjour* (good day) all day long to say hello, but switch to *bonsoir* (good evening) in the evening. When saying goodbye, use *au revoir* (to the seeing again). On non-business occasions it is common for men and women to kiss each other on the cheek (or just in the air) 3 to 4 times. Observe the local custom.

In the Italian part, people greet each other in the morning with *Buongiorno* (good day) and with *Buonasera* (good evening) in the afternoon. When leaving, they use *Arrivederci* (to the seeing again).

A Word of Advice

English has no formal and informal forms, and thus the degree of formality when addressing somebody is often conveyed by the use of the first name. As the line between Mr. Smith and William is not clear-cut as in French, German or Italian, people are often more relaxed in using first names. Do not try to call a Swiss by his or her first name unless you are invited to or know this person very well. Although the person you are talking to might understand that your intention is to be friendly but not impolite, it will probably cause some discomfort nonetheless.

Communication Styles

Nonverbal communication

Basic nonverbal communication rules are not very different in Switzerland than in other Northwestern European countries. Leaning forward means agreement, whereas leaning backward indicates suspicion. Crossing the arms is a sign of closure, meaning that the person disagrees or is bored. People nod their head vertically to mean yes and sideways to mean no.

When talking, the Swiss won't become excited and will never do big gestures. If they keep quiet, that doesn't mean a lack of enthusiasm. The Swiss will never reveal right away what they are really thinking. They are too scared to say something that you may not be ready to hear or that might make you uneasy. They will first try to gain your trust. Then they will beat around the bush a little to determine the best way to tell you what is really on their mind. When they explain something to you, they will try to judge by the reaction of your face if you approve, asking for an answer by smiling. You should definitely participate in this little game if you want to have a more in-depth conversation with whomever you are speaking.

Joking With the Swiss

The educated Swiss are very witty and often deliberately say things that have many meanings. Their humor is very intellectual and should at least make you smile. It is a sort of rite of initiation. If you are able to understand it and answer intelligently, the Swiss will consider you one of their own.

You should certainly not be offended by these battles of wit or pretend not to have understood. It is in your best interest to respond with a humorous line of the same genre. This tit-for-tat response will not only flatter the person with whom you are talking, but will also show that you appreciate their sort of subtleties and demonstrate that you have a good understanding of things and do not need to have them explained to you. The Swiss appreciate being able to say things without explaining them.

If the Swiss feel that you are on the same wave length they will not hesitate to imply certain more serious information that they would not have been able, out of modesty, to tell you directly. Discreetly continue to show that you follow their train of thought and they will open themselves up willingly.

On the other hand, outbursts of laughter are not recommended. In fact, over-emotionalism is considered a sign of weakness. Try to avoid being too publicly affectionate. Never shout or speak loudly. The Swiss will always wait to be near you to greet you. Only the young or the impolite wave or shout at each other from far away.

Small Talk

In certain cultures it is considered taboo to talk about the weather as it is seen as conversation piece of last resort or a lack of willingness to talk about other things. In Switzerland, however, you should not be shocked if this topic comes up time and again, especially at the beginning of conversations. This makes for a light beginning to a discussion and avoids jumping into the heart of any given topic that might make either person uncomfortable. The country's landscape makes for dramatic climatic variations, even over short distances. The weather forecast is obviously one of the most frequently watched programs as the Swiss love discussing the climatic differences between the regions of the Alps, the Jura (mountains between France and Switzerland), and the plains.

The Art of Consensus

One of the most prominent aspects of Swiss culture is its incessant attempts to achieve consensus. This modus vivendi is determined by the extremely heterogeneous population: 26 cantons, 4 national languages, 2 major religions, a clear division between urban and rural areas—all doubled by the distinction between the Alps and the plains. So many differences which miraculously do not become destabilizing factors! On the contrary, everyone is aware of the respect due to others as well as their opinions.

At the political level, the decision-making process revolves around the need to consider all of the concerns of the respective groups. The people most affected by a decision are always consulted beforehand. The numerous associations and televised Sunday morning debates, which invite representatives from all walks of life, are considered fundamental institutions as they contribute to the political decision-making process. Rather than letting ideas take their own course, an attempt is made to find a common position that could accommodate the masses. Everyone is, therefore, forced to make certain compromises.

These negotiations take time, often a lot of time. After all, it is said that the Swiss are slow. But when the decision has been taken, it encounters no obstacles once it has been set in motion. In fact, these discussions allow for a solution perfectly adapted to the reality of the problem to be reached. As the groups who would be mainly affected by the decision participate in the negotiations, they are convinced that the solution arrived at is the most reasonable. And the minority whose rights may have been infringed, is, in most cases, awarded compensation.

The consecration of this culture of consensus can be found in the collegial form of executive and federal power and in most of the cantonal governments. A group of 7 "counselors" make up the federal government. Each member of the "college" defends his or her point of view behind closed doors. Then discussions are held to determine a common or at least a majority opinion. Once a decision has been made all the members of the college are required to defend it publicly regardless of their initial opinion. They become little more than spokespeople for the government as a whole. Politicians who wish to distance themselves from the collective decision taken with their colleagues will immediately become pariahs, a fact that goes to show just how important this process is to the peace of this very heterogeneous country.

Therefore, do not be surprised if it takes a long

time to decide on business matters. The Swiss will first try to find out the opinions of those concerned. They will then try to rally the interest of the majority around a common project, as this has proven to be the only viable long-term solution. It would be very surprising if a decision were made based on a brainstorming session or against the will of the majority.

Direct confrontations are completely counter-productive, not to mention socially unacceptable in Switzerland. If you want your ideas to be incorporated into the final product, it is better to ensure a dominating position by taking an active role in the project development by contributing constructively in the discussions. Trying to use blackmail or pressure after the fact will have no effect at all. As the decision reached is the fruit of a collective work, everyone involved will unite to save their laborious equilibrium.

Cleanliness

The Swiss have always considered themselves to be like a *Sonderfall* (an exception). They smile indulgently about their French neighbors with their unwashed houses, unorganized cities, massive strikes, unstable politics and badly run businesses. Until recently Italy and Spain were judged even more severely, that is to say, almost as if they were third world countries. But the Swiss do not consider themselves to be overly fanatic in any way. Only the Germans are fanatics. The Swiss are disciplined.

Manners and Politeness

The Swiss are extremely polite. Expressions like "thank you very much" or "my pleasure" are used all the time. Car drivers are very courteous with pedestrians. If they notice that someone wants to cross the street, they will stop and give a hand signal to the pedestrian indicating that he or she can cross safely. The pedestrian, out of gratitude, should respond by a hand signal or a quick glance accompanied by a nod of the head.

In small cities, villages, and on mountain trails, it is customary to greet people you pass (even if you do not know them) with a cordial *Gruezi* (hello) or *Bonjour* (good day). In cities, this gesture is still used when entering stores or small cafés. It is considered equally civil to give your seat to senior citizens and pregnant women on public transportation.

Even if it is true that women appreciate good manners, you should not try too hard to impress them. It is up to you to judge how much chivalry a woman expects. But be careful not to make her feel childish or relegate her to a position of inferiority. Swiss women also enjoy their independence and many of them no longer appreciate the paternalistic aspect of courtesy.

If a woman insists on sharing the bill or treating you to dinner, you can protest politely but go along with it. She will feel as though you see her as an equal and will feel satisfied that she does not owe you anything.

Customs

Celebrations and Religion

Catholicism (43.6% of the population) and Protestantism (50.4%) have left their mark on Swiss society and continue to do so today.

Even if Christian values are turning less and less to ecclesiastic institutions as a means of expression, Churches and the Christian perspective remain a stabilizing factor of the society. At the same time, there is a more pronounced tendency towards individual interpretation of religion, and the interest in new forms of religion and spirituality is growing.

Many see in the Swiss work ethic, their reserved nature and realist outlook, an influence of Protestant values with the stamp of Calvinism. If economic thought has its foundations in Protestantism, then it is perhaps the Catholic tradition that gave the Swiss character its strong ties to the land and its love for rural traditions and ritual festivities.

The year passes by to the rhythm of the holidays. Here are some examples of Switzerland's most famous.

National Day

If it's true that you can judge a country's image of itself by its National Day, then Switzerland definitely offers a relaxing sight. No military parades and no grandiose speeches on *Lebensraum* (living space).

On August the first, the whole country gathers in public places around bonfires and listens to speeches about the independence of the country from the Austrian rulers, which started with the Grütli Pact of 1291.

The first of August is celebrated solely in the municipalities. Only one radio and television broadcast of a speech by the President of the Confederation currently in office reminds the Swiss that their cities are united in cantons, which in turn makes the Helvetic Confederation. Thought-provoking words from an eminent cultural or political speaker, songs and music, gymnastic shows and group performances of the Swiss national anthem are the traditional elements of the holiday.

Many municipalities set off fireworks, and these spectacular light shows are often ignited from the mountains and hills. They serve as a reminder of the expulsion of the foreign bailiffs in the 14th century, for the great news was announced in this very way. The children march through the streets at dusk with candle-lit Chinese lanterns. Flags with the arms of the Confederation, the canton and the municipality fly proudly above public and private buildings alike. Even the bakers get involved, decorating their rolls of bread with little Swiss flags.

The holiday takes on a whole new dimension at Neuhausen am Rheinfall in the Canton of Schaffhouse, with the illumination of the 25-meter high Rhine waterfalls. This extravaganza is completed by a great fireworks display that draws throngs of spectators. And, like everywhere else, speeches, songs, music and the national anthem animate the evening.

The Carnival of Basle

The Carnival of Basle is the largest popular festival in Switzerland, gathering between 10,000 and 20,000 costume-clad participants each year.

The famous opening call, known as the *Morgenstreich*, is sounded the Monday after Ash Wednesday at four o'clock in the morning. Fife players and drummers, bedecked and masked, set off swaying to the heart of the city that awaits their arrival in the darkness. The bands of bugles and drums carry lanterns that can reach up to 3 meters in height, creations of wood and fabric that are lit from within and parody the events of the past year.

For four days, the *Guggenmuusige* (masked street orchestras) liven up the city with their incessant parade. The merry-making will last until Thursday at four in the morning—and then it's another year of patience until the long-awaited sounding of the Morgenstreich.

The Neuchatel Wine Festival

Vines have been cultivated on the Neuchatel hillsides for over ten centuries now, so it comes as no surprise that the people of Neuchatel celebrate its harvest with a colorful wine festival.

And celebration it is! From Friday to Sunday, day and night, stands and refreshment booths jam-pack the squares and streets of the city center, serving food and drink for the thousands of spectators who come to unwind and admire the parades and decorations. The children's procession takes place on Saturday afternoon, followed by a parade of local or guest marching bands in the evening.

The highlight of the festival is the big Sunday afternoon parade. Local businesses sponsor countless carnival floats that are decorated with flowers and parade through the streets of the city, united by a common theme. To the beat of the brass bands, and accompanied by groups in costume, this procession is keeping tradition alive as it recalls the stream of wine-grower's wagons passing through the town after the harvest, decorated and adorned with garlands, and loaded with all their work tools.

The Bern Onion Market

On the fourth Sunday in November, the old city in Bern, between the railway station and the Place du Palais fédéral (Bundesplatz), blossoms into a giant market with hundreds of stalls. Neighboring farmers gather to sell over 100 tons of plaited strings of onions, as well as other fruits, vegetables and nuts, while street venders and secondhand goods dealers peddle their traditional wares. In the afternoon and evening, especially after school and work, the carnival-side of the festival, with confetti fights and people in costume, melds with the lively market scene. In the evening, ironic poetry recitals on the events of the past year are held in the local taverns. Satirical newspapers are also published on Onion Market day.

The Valais Cow Fights

Traditional cow fights take place throughout the region where the Eringer breed is raised (Central Valais, Lower Valais, and the Aoste Valley in Northern Italy). More than other breeds of cow, these small, but hearty black creatures with short robust horns have retained the hierarchical organization that is instinctive to any animal society.

Thus, at the start of spring, they battle amongst themselves to determine the pecking order for leading the herd to summer in the high mountain pastures.

The fights don't occur in an organized fashion: each cow spontaneously chooses its opponent. However, competitions have been held in the last several years to determine the Queen of the region or canton. Live national television broadcasts of these folkloric competitions have met with great success. For it's true that each battle is quite an impressive sight: the cow stops grazing, lowers its head, snorts noisily and scrapes the ground with its hind hooves. If a cow of equal strength takes up the challenge, it will move towards the first with the same snorting and scraping. The approach is slow and careful. The fight begins in a fury, heads knock, horns lock, each cow searching for a good hold. Then they lean in and press with all their might, advancing and retreating with each gust of strength. After a battle, which can last anywhere up to several minutes, the loser does an about face and runs away, with its victorious rival in hot pursuit striking out with a few more jabs of the horns.

Culture

French-speaking Swiss are believed to be different from German-speaking Swiss because the former have something of France and the latter have something of Germany. The people of Uri differ from the people of Ticino, so it's said, because the first live on the shady slopes of their mountains and the others live on the sunny shores of their lakes. But what do they share, apart from their Swiss passports? C.F. Ramuz, one of Switzerland's best known francophone authors, describes the situation as follows: "it's an overwhelming task to try to describe a people, especially when they don't exist. For those of us who are, we know very well that we are not Swiss. We come from Neuchatel, like you, or the Vaud, like me, or from Valais, or Zurich, meaning that we are citizens of our own mini countries..." The only uniformity in Switzerland lies in our mailboxes and our army uniforms. Everywhere else, we carefully distinguish ourselves from one another. And the greatest irony of it all is that in the end, these precautionary measures lead to us to being asked when traveling abroad: "Hey, you're Swiss? How is it that you speak French so well?"

When asked what they love about their country, the majority of Swiss will first mention the beautiful landscape. They think of a hilly countryside dotted with isolated farms or sleepy little villages, forests dressed in autumn colors and majestic mountains.

To be sure, the mountains play a vital part in the image the Swiss have of themselves and their country. The Swiss population is said to have a "rural" mentality, rural being understood as a certain love of the land, nature and traditions—characteristics considered to be rural, even though sixty percent of the population works in the service industry and the majority are purely urban.

In the harsh life of earlier times, people had no choice but to think things through and plan ahead. Nothing grew on its own, the soil needed to be worked constantly, diligently. The heedless were rewarded in kind, for the soil was not rich in natural resources. Since arable land was limited between the mountains, people had to measure carefully, economize, partition off and distribute. The mountains and hills made contact difficult: the people stayed amongst themselves and depended on one another for help.

Time has long past since the Swiss were so dependent on the climate, nature and the topography of the land. Mountains are no longer obstacles. But the ability to anticipate and plan ahead is considered a virtue among the Swiss to this day. Hard work is still appreciated and the people are apt to cling to what is near, to what seems useful, nurturing and perfecting what they have and ensuring that everything is in good order.

The Swiss like everything to remain within reasonable proportions. No blade of grain ought to stick out above the rest: that's the rule. It is best to be serious and reliable rather than brilliant and original. They aren't particularly keen on extravagance. They seek out a consensus, compromise.

The results of a recent survey conducted on young people associated the following characteristics with the Swiss: serious, rich and sincere (75%); fair (66%), social (40%); satisfied, optimistic (40%); lively, imaginative (20%); generous (12%).

Gifts

A bottle of wine is the standard gift when invited for dinner to someone's home. As explained in the business gifts section, good Swiss chocolates are always welcome, although you should be discerning when offering such in the country with the highest per capita chocolate consumption in the world. The best would be handcrafted chocolate coming from a small shop making small batches of high quality product. Do not purchase and give any of the big brand name chocolate products. The Swiss are usually very interested in other countries and if you have brought something from your country this is even better. However, offering Belgium chocolate is a no-no.

 Dress & Appearance

The Swiss can be remarkably casual in their dress, save for the highest-ranking management. Also, people have been known to sport tasteless ties (lilac or gray) with watercolor suits (green or burgundy are a common sight among middle management). Several banks recently banned white socks with business suits in their dress codes.

Business Attire

In upper management, corporate finance and private banks, dark suits are the rule as in many countries. In most other industries you will encounter countless types of attire. Lower-ranking employees often wear casual clothes and jeans are quite common.

The Swiss may be admired for a few things, but clothing is probably not among them. Most striking is a style sometimes described as the "Swiss German style," which the author of this book recently had the privilege of observing on a live specimen: greenish suit, pink shirt, brown shoes, a superb tie covered with bright flowers—the kind you see on shower curtains—and, the finishing touch, a pair of glasses with heavy blue plastic frames.

Shoes

The first thing the Swiss look at to judge someone's credibility is the condition of their shoes. Always try to have good shoes that are well polished (never running shoes) if you want to leave a good impression. On the same note, clean nails reveal that you are a well-groomed person. The Swiss hold that if people make an effort to take good care of themselves, they will also make an effort in doing business.

Ethnic Clothing

On weekends you might bump into people wearing the full folkloric attire of their region. Chances are that they are on their way to a music celebration somewhere in the mountains. Women often carry flower baskets and men popular musical instruments like the Alp Horn, which can be heard from mountain to mountain.

Reading the Swiss

Reserved People

There won't be much to read on your Swiss acquaintances at first. Private bankers and Palace employees are best known to be unreadable, accustomed as they are to their eccentric rich clients. Tell them you think it's blue and they will agree. Change your mind and say that, no, after all you believe it's red, and they will revise their opinion accordingly. But after some time you will recognize the meaning behind their "Really?" and raised eyebrows.

Gestures and Expressions

Always shake hands when being introduced to a Swiss, and when leaving. This is standard behavior, even with young and casual people.

It is also customary to greet the proprietor upon entering a shop, bar or café, and to say goodbye when leaving.

Public displays of affection are fine, but are more common in French-speaking Switzerland than in the slightly more formal German-speaking parts. Exchanging kisses (three times, alternating cheeks) upon meeting is a common ritual in French-speaking Switzerland.

At the dinner table, everybody waits for the host to make a toast prior to drinking, and before your impatient lips stretch for that soothing libation you must clink glasses with everyone present while looking into their eyes. Before tucking into the food, the cry of *en Guete* or *Bon Appétit* is heard.

Most Swiss go to bed early, so don't overstay your welcome if you are invited to somebody's home and don't telephone anyone after about 9 P.M.

Don't flaunt your wealth and don't talk about salaries. What a person makes is nobody's business. Even amongst friends it is rarely discussed. Switzerland is a wealthy country and the majority of the population lives comfortably, but some are richer than others. They are no less modest, however, and they do not put their riches on display. Fritz Zorn, the writer from the *Goldenküste* (the posh Zurich lake shore neighborhood) explains: "In my home, the way we minimized anything that had to do with money was typically Swiss. We had possessions, but we didn't show it. Nothing was flashy or showy; solidity was what mattered. Quite often things that didn't look like much had cost a fortune. We didn't serve caviar on gold plates. Rather, we ate soup in bowls that one would think came from ABM [Swiss department store], but actually cost us a thousand francs a piece." (Fritz Zorn, *Mars*)

19 Entertaining

Swiss Food

Swiss food is not the first reason to come to Switzerland. Hearty dishes come from the country agricultural background, with many made from cheese. Fondue is basically melted cheese in a boiling casserole in which you dip pieces of bread with a long fork. Everybody shares the same pot in this solid dish. Raclette used to be a shepherd's dish and is prepared by melting the side of a cut cheese (about 5 kg) on an oven. Each guest eats a cut of melted cheese in turn with potatoes and pickles until he has eaten his fill. Adding salt or mustard is a no-no and experienced raclette eaters always taste the cheese before adding pepper.

The paragon dish of Swiss German-speaking Switzerland is the *rösti* (pronounced rush-T), roasted potatoes with cheese or bacon on top.

When choosing a restaurant, always ask a local for advice or look in a knowledgeable guidebook. Picking the first restaurant you find is a sure way to eat an overpriced and dull meal. If you are in Western Switzerland, it is often worth crossing the border and eating in a French restaurant: prices in France are about 40% lower and the food is usually a lot better. This is, however, usually not the case in Germany if you happen to be close to its border.

However, you should not think that just because Swiss food has no pretension to beat Italian or French standards, Swiss cooks have given up hopes of being world class. The leading hostelry schools are in Switzerland and the highbrow French food guide Gault-Millaut gave its best award to no less than 7 Swiss restaurants.

Wine

Switzerland produces excellent wines, especially in Vaud and Valais. In the latter, most people have a small vineyard in their family and they either produce their own wine or receive bottles from the family plot. Being invited in a *carnotzet* (underground cellar where men meet) to taste your host's wine and eat some dried meat and cheese is a great honor and should not be refused.

Table Manners

Always wait for everybody to be served before beginning to eat. If wine is served, you should usually chink glasses with everybody at the table before taking the first sip. When you are over, put your knife and fork on the plate as if they were clock hands indicating 5:25 P.M. If you don't, your host will serve you more.

Eating at Swiss Restaurants

Most Swiss restaurants serve international dishes, often of French inspiration. In the middle price range there are scores of pizzerias, usually reliably good Italian restaurants serving Italian-style pizza and pasta.

People often show up at 6:30 P.M. for dinner, and by 10 P.M. most restaurants are half-empty. Eating out after 11 P.M. is a challenge even in fast foods.

Food and service are sometimes less than perfect in Swiss restaurants, although prices are always high, so if you are not satisfied with your meal, you should not hesitate to complain to the maître d'hôtel.

Check and Tips

"Going Dutch," or paying separately, is to be avoided for business lunches. Whoever has done the other a favor is supposed to pay for the lunch. For example, if somebody has offered you some free advice or has bought you something, then you should pick up the tab. Of course the situation is sometimes unclear. In such cases, it is common to alternate the invitation, with your acquaintance paying this time and you the next. If you intend to pay the next time, make it clear diplomatically.

Service is always included in Switzerland, and tips are often given only if you had outstanding service. People customarily give 1 to 5 francs for meals, although Middle Eastern tourists sometimes tip hundreds of francs.

20 Socializing

Reading the Neue Zürcher Zeitung (NZZ)

For upper class German-speaking Swiss, the newspaper of reference is without a doubt their beloved NZZ. And there's some ground for this fondness, although you won't find it in its conservative layout, where the editor seems to be keen on choosing the dullest pictures (never more than one per page). Here the name of the game is content, thoroughly researched and as *seriös* as can be. Sentences often stretch over 7 lines (with the verb coming last) and tables are preferred to graphs. One of the oldest newspapers in the world, the NZZ has been the main body of the Swiss liberal movement for over 220 years.

But this is a world-class newspaper, with 180 full time journalists, more than half of who are *Doktor*, and with over 45 foreign correspondents. People who can read German appreciate its independent stance on international political and economic analysis. As the leading business paper of a small country, the NZZ can cast a much more liberal eye on other nations' issues, and usually does

great insight. Its daily international edi-
~~/~~ublished in over 100 countries across five
~~nts~~. For those who don't read German,
NZZ Online (www.nzz.ch) has an "English Win-
dow" link featuring English translations of their
best articles.

Associations

In Switzerland, the best way to gain some
political and social clout is to create an association.
There are associations for everything, from the
trade guilds to the association of chocolate eaters.
These groups can become extremely influential,
even more than the political parties. The best example would have to be the ASIN, the Association for
a Switzerland Independent and Neutral, a conservative group that could easily collect 100,000 signatures to put to vote any law they happen to
disapprove of.

The Swiss political system lends so such
weight to the various interest groups and associations that political scientists are now referring to a
consociational democracy. They play a fundamental role in development of legislation that serves
their interests.

This associative phenomenon is one of the cor-
nerstones of Swiss culture, the legacy of a long tradition of communal life. Joining an association is an
excellent way for a foreigner to socialize. It's often
said that when three Swiss meet in a bistro, they rep-
resent the President, Secretary and Treasurer of a
budding association. It begins early, with the *Société
de Jeunesse*, or youth club, a typically Swiss group
that brings together single youth from the time they
finish their compulsory schooling (around 16 years)
up until marriage. In the last few years, young
women have been admitted into these clubs,

although they used to be strictly men-only affairs.

Each village also has a firefighter's association, made up entirely of volunteers who ensure safekeeping at the sound of the alarm.

And then of course there is the ever-present brass band that gathers together inhabitants from all areas, true lovers of military or civil music. This group is inevitably in charge of village animation, and you will be sure to find them at any event that deals with village life.

Singing Swiss

The Swiss love to sing. Not while they work, like the Italian painters or Portuguese vine growers, and not necessarily in public, but in the intimacy of a meeting hall. Song is a way for these discreet people to express their feelings. Rare is the village in all of Switzerland that doesn't have its own choir: *Männerchor* or *Jodlerclub* (men's choir or yodeling club) in German-speaking Switzerland, mixed choirs in French-speaking Switzerland, *canzone* in Ticino. Choir members meet once a week, generally in the back room of a restaurant or in the parish hall, and they tirelessly rehearse the songs they will perform at a regional, cantonal or federal festival, where they are often dressed in traditional costumes. Their repertoire varies according to region and the tastes of the director, often including folk songs, specially adapted modern tunes, and sometimes works written by classical musicians.

Several Swiss composers regularly add to the repertoire of these choral groups, since they play such a vital socio-cultural role throughout the country. The most famous of these composers is the abbot Joseph Bovet, who wrote several folk songs that made their way past the Swiss borders. He is behind the adaptation of the famous *Ranz des vaches*, (the March of the Cows in the Fribourg French dialect), which is akin to a national anthem for the francophone Swiss who know all the lyrics by heart. In simple words, the song tells of a herd of cattle making its way down from the mountain pastures to the village...

Music & Film Festivals

Even though the Swiss are not generally considered to be festive, music festivals are an exception. Such festivals usually take place in the summer and attract people from all over the country. For classical music, the most famous is the Lucerne festival. The city built a brand new auditorium for the festival. Designed by French architect Jean Nouvelle, the building on the lakeshore can be seen from everywhere in the city. Every year, thousands of people come to Lucerne to hear the best interpretation of the moment, and the contagious festive atmosphere spreads throughout the city.

Since its beginnings as a three-day event in 1967, the Montreux Jazz Festival has become a stupendous 16-day affair, headlined by jazz, blues, rock, world-music and soul luminaries such as George Benson, Maria Bethania, Ray Charles, Eric Clapton, Miles Davis, Ella Fitzgerald, Roberta Flack, Aretha Franklin, Herbie Hancock, Etta James, Quincy Jones, B. B. King, Oscar Peterson and Sting. Festival founder Claude Nobs created an event that was to become one of the most important festivals of all, with a unique and eclectic musical reputation. Every year, up to 200,000 visitors attend the Festival at the prestigious Auditorium Stravinski and in the festive atmosphere of the Miles Davis Hall, or enjoy the numerous free concerts at the Festival-Off that are held from one end of Montreux to the other. The lake plays its due part as well, being host to the Bahia Boat, where Brazilian music lovers can enjoy the one and only "carnival on water." And then a week later, "little bro," the Memphis Boat, offers a slightly "jazzier" cruise. As for the Montreux Jazz Café, it is the place to spend the last hours of the night in an avant-garde atmosphere. Internationally renowned DJs light up the place every evening, partying until dawn.

Locarno, where the Cinema has been celebrated for fifty years, lies on the shores of Lake Maggiore in southern Switzerland (the Ticino Canton). Although at the foot of the Alps, it enjoys a pleasant, Mediterranean climate. Locarno has long attracted political and cultural personalities from across Europe. The Locarno International Film Festival upholds the city's tradition as a meeting place for people from all over the world. Traditionally devoted to the promotion of new filmmakers and new movements, the Festival has contributed to showcasing or confirming directors who are currently enjoying wide recognition. The event draws 150,000 viewers each year.

Taboos in Conversation

All countries have skeletons in their closets, historical or otherwise. You should keep clear of some topics when schmoozing with your Swiss hosts. Take WWII. Although most Swiss are now aware of the ambiguous role their country played during WWII, they are reluctant to talk about it and even more with a foreigner. Don't ask why Switzerland lost the 2004 Olympic Winter games to Italy, nor what happened to the Marcos millions and your conversation will run smoothly. There is a Swiss proverb that sums up the attitude one ought to adopt: *On ne parle pas de corde dans la maison du pendu.* (One should not talk about rope in the hanged man's home.) Here is some background on two of the major taboos for foreigners to discuss with the Swiss.

Switzerland during WWII

No European country remained truly neutral during WWII. Portugal, Spain, Sweden and Switzerland all worked to some extent with the Axis. In Switzerland, the people who lived through the war wanted to believe that it was their army and fortifications that kept the Nazis out. Historical research and documents clearly show that if the Nazis wanted to invade Switzerland, it would have been quick and relatively easy. The reason Germany spared its tiny neighbor to the south was because Switzerland proved much more useful as an independent state than as a satellite. The Swiss made many useful weapon components (aluminium for the Luftwaffe, spark plugs for jeeps taken from the Russians, timing devices for bombs, among other things), and thus their factories were not bombed every night. The Swiss National bank bought gold from the Reichsbank, the Reichsbank was given Swiss francs in exchange, and used them to buy cobalt, nickel and tungsten from the other "neutral" countries. The Turks, Portuguese, Spanish and Swedish, who were all under heavy pressure from the Allies not to accept direct gold payment from the Reichsbank, then exchanged the Swiss francs for gold. The problem was that the German gold came from the Belgian National bank reserves (not from concentration camps as some sensationalists would have it) and the neutrals knew it. Finally, the Swiss allowed trains to carry food and non-weapon supplies from Germany to Italy, with dozens of trains every day on their way to Africa.

But did Switzerland have any other choice?

Probably not. Totally surrounded by the Axis, most of its coal supply came from Germany every week, and all of its exports had to go through Axis controlled territory. For a landlocked country with no natural resources, this meant the Swiss had to work out some form of accomodation with their neighbors.

The problem is that the postwar generations have been raised to believe that it was the Swiss army, and not the country's usefulness to the Germans, that protected it from the wrath of war. The Swiss are now coming to terms with this part of their history, as for example the people of France and Japan have. As a foreigner, it is best to avoid passing judgment on them and giving lessons, at the risk of offending your hosts.

Dormant Accounts and Banking Scandals

Swiss banking is no small business, and bankers levy a considerable amount of power in Switzerland. This does not protect them from making very foolish errors. In the late 1930s, Swiss bankers pushed for a law to be passed forbidding any bank employee from disclosing information about a client. This was the formal birth of Swiss banking secrecy, a practice born in the late 18th century to protect the wealth of French aristocrats fleeing the Revolution. The laws were passed to give added protection to the people fleeing a government that increasingly looted individuals from their assets, Nazi Germany.

Thousands of people deposited their savings, big and small, into Swiss banks, so that whatever happened to them, their money would be safe for their offspring. Many of those depositors were never seen again, and years afterwards people came calling on the banks to reclaim their parents' assets. The bankers asked them to prove that original depositors were deceased and that they were the legitimate heirs, which was often impossible for people whose parents had died in concentration camps.

Now begins the painful part. Instead of actively looking for the legitimate owners of the money, the banks just stood there, hiding behind banking secrecy to say that they could not publish a list of dormant account holder names.

In the late 1990s, the scandal broke out, with several international Jewish organizations filing class-action lawsuits in the US against the Swiss banks. The Swiss banks reacted very poorly and in the end were forced to pay $1.25 billion on top of all the money found in dormant accounts.

The Swiss people recognize that the banks behaved in an irresponsible and inept way in the handling of both the dormant accounts and the latter scandal. However, many Swiss also have the bitter impression that some Jewish organizations have used a good cause to get both money and publicity at the expense of the Swiss, taking advantage of the US litigation system. In addition, they also feel that most of the other countries that surround Switzerland have similar skeletons in the WWII closet, yet have never suffered the same humiliating media attacks worldwide. Some think that Switzerland has been used as an example for bigger countries (such as France) that could not be treated in such a fashion.

Whatever your knowledge of these topics, you are strongly advised against starting a discussion about them with your Swiss acquaintances.

Basic Phrases

English	German	French	Italian
Yes	Ja	Oui	Si
No	Nein	Non	No
Good morning	Gut Morgen	Bonjour	Buongiorno
Hello (daytime)	Guten Tag	Bonjour	Buongiorno
Hello (evening)	Guten Abend	Bonsoir	Buonasera
Hello (phone)	Hallo	Allo	Pronto
Goodbye	Auf wiedersehen	Au-revoir	Arrivederci
Goodnight	Gute Nacht	Bonne nuit	Buona notte
Please	Bitte	S'il vous plaît	Per favore
Thank you	Danke	Merci	Grazie

English	German	French	Italian
Excuse me	Entschuldig-ung	Excusez-moi	Scusi
Do you speak English?	Sprechen Sie English?	Vous parlez anglais?	Parla inglese?
My name is...	Ich heisse	Je m'appelle	Mi chiamo
I don't understand	Ich verstehe es nicht	Je ne comprends pas	Non capisco
How much is it?	Wieviel kostet?	Combien cela coûte-t-il?	Cuanto costa?
I don't speak German/French/Italian.	Ich spreche nicht Deutsch.	Je ne parle pas français.	Non parlo italiano.
What's your name?	Wie heissen Sie ?	Comment vous appelez-vous ?	Lei come si chiama ?
Nice to meet you.	Sehr erfreut.	Enchanté	Piacere
Sorry	Verzeihung	Désolé	Mi dispiace
How are you?	Wie geht es Ihnen?	Comment allez-vous ?	Come sta ?

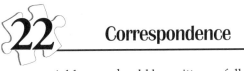

22 Correspondence

Addresses should be written as follows:

Herr
François Micheloud
Micheloud & Cie
Grand-Chêne 8
Postfach 3332
CH-1003 LAUSANNE
Switzerland

In German, Herr means Mister and usually occupies a line by itself. If the letter is addressed to a company, the correct term is Firma (on its own line as well).

In French, you should write Monsieur or Madame (don't abbreviate). GmbH or A.G. (in German) and S.A. (in French) means it's a corporation.

The street name is followed by the street number.

CH stands for Confederatio Helveticae (official name of Switzerland). The name of the city is capitalized. Don't underline it. If there's a Post Office Box, write Postfach (German) or Case Postale (French), followed by the number.

23 Useful Telephone Numbers

To call Switzerland from outside the country you must use your country's international access code followed by the Swiss country code [41] and don't dial the "0" area code prefix. If dialing within Switzerland, use the "0" area code prefix if you are not in the same region. Don't dial the area code if you are in the same region.

Police and Emergency 117
Fire department 118
Ambulance & Medical Team 144
Swiss Federal Railway hotline 157
Regional codes: Zurich: 01, Geneva: 022
Basle: 061, Lausanne: 021
Bern: 031, Valais: 027
International operator (English-speaking) . 1141
Local telephone directory assistance 111
International telephone directory assistance:
- for Austria 1151
- for Germany 1152
- for France 1153
- for Italy 1154
- for other countries 1159
Tourist information . . . . (0) 1 288 11 11

24 Books & Internet Addresses

Books

Xenophobe's guide to the Swiss, by Paul Bilton, 1999 (ISBN: 1902825454). Despite its quirky name, this is one of the best books in print if you're looking for a witty introduction to the Swiss people.

Living and Working in Switzerland, edited by David Hampshire, 2000 (ISBN: 1901130169). This book is packed with facts you'll want to know if you are considering moving to Switzerland. Everything, from details about residence permits, to the cost of every conceivable type of train pass, to minutiae about language are included.

Why Switzerland? by Jonathan Steinberg, 1996 (ISBN: 0521481708). This book does a very good job of explaining the origins and dynamics of modern Switzerland. This is not a travel book, rather an examination of Swiss politics, history and culture.

Ticking along with the Swiss, by Diana Dicks, Bergli Books, 1998 (ISBN: 3952000248). This popular book contains a delightful collection of personal experiences of English-speaking writers, journalists, translators, teachers and business people of many different nationalities who live and work with the Swiss. They record their impressions, wonder, perplexity and assimilation in essays, poems, anecdotes and letters.

The Rough Guide to Switzerland by Matthew Teller, 2000 (ISBN 1-85828-538-0). In our opinion, the best travel guide about Switzerland currently in print, with over 500 pages of exhaustive descriptions of Switzerland's numerous tourist attractions. The book has been thoroughly researched and contains a lot of historical and cultural information in an easy-to-read format.

Switzerland: Land People Economy, by Aubrey Diem, 1994 (ISBN: 0969229178). Based on the author's 40 years of research and field experience in Switzerland, the text covers and analyzes the history, economy, population, transportation, cities, and regions of the country.

Internet Addresses

Immigration to Switzerland and corporate services
www.switzerland.isyours.com
Swiss Tourism Association
www.switzerlandtourism.ch
Swiss Federal Railways
www.cff.ch
Live pictures from Switzerland
www.topin.ch/ch/
Swiss information and communication
www.switzerland-in-sight.ch
Swiss bank accounts
www.swiss-bank-accounts.com
Swiss Firms Database
www.swissfirms.ch

Usenet Groups

soc.culture.swiss
ch.talk
ch.rec

François Micheloud, a Swiss living in the Lake Geneva area, is a specialist in financial, corporate and personal relocation to Switzerland. His firm takes care of the needs of companies and wealthy individuals who want to establish a presence in Switzerland, assisting them in matters of residence permits, taxes, real estate, recruitment, banking, etc. He holds graduate degrees in Economics and Sociology and is fluent in six languages.